Ogres Awake!

James Sturm
Andrew Arnold
Alexis Frederick-Frost

FETCH, EDWARD!

:01
First Second
New York

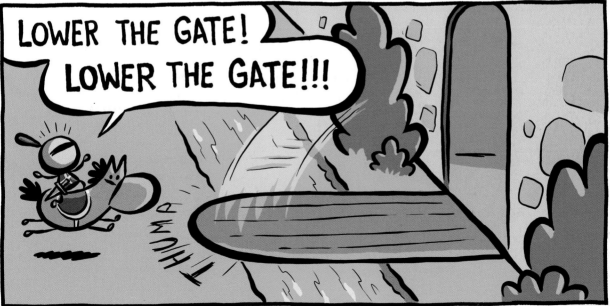

First Second
New York

Published by First Second
First Second is an imprint of Roaring Brook Press, a division of
Holtzbrinck Publishing Holdings Limited Partnership
175 Fifth Avenue, New York, New York 10010
All rights reserved

Library of Congress Control Number: 2015944388

ISBN: 978-1-59643-653-4

Our books may be purchased in bulk for promotional, educational, or business use.
Please contact your local bookseller or the Macmillan Corporate and Premium Sales Department
at (800) 221-7945 ext. 5422 or by email at MacmillanSpecialMarkets@macmillan.com.

 First edition 2016
Printed in China by Macmillan Production (Asia) Ltd.,
Kowloon Bay, Hong Kong (Vendor Code: 10)

1 3 5 7 9 10 8 6 4 2

BY ART
WE LIVE

OGRES AWAKE was drawn and colored in Adobe Photoshop using a Wacom tablet.
Text was hand-lettered on Vellum paper using Staedtler pigment liner pens.

DRAW THE GNOMES!

Step 1

Step 2

Step 3

Step 4

Step 5

Step 6

Step 7

Step 8

Struttin'

Dancing

Plowing

Doin' the Heisman

Happy

NOT Happy

Sleepy

Wise